Locked In Love

Channeled Messages from Spirit

Ingrid Turner

INGRID TURNER

ISBN: 0692983279
ISBN-13: 978-0692983270

DEDICATION

When asked for a dedication for this book, I nearly opted out entirely. There are far too many people who have assisted me and inspired me along my path to list on just one page – or even several.

But I re-thought it, and realized that, while everyone who has crossed my path on this tremendous journey with Spirit deserves my utmost thanks and appreciation, there are a few people who, if not for their unwavering support and grounding guidance at the very beginning of this often insane journey, I would not be sitting and writing this today.

I know this to be true. So, I name the few, just this once.

First, my mother, Vilina Hutter, needs mention and my deepest thanks. I'm not sure I've ever really given her that due. As I stepped off the cliff of Spirit, she was at the other end of every ecstatic and haphazard phone call, listening, and not calling the authorities to have me committed. Thanks Mama. Truly. You are an invaluable support to me.

Lisa Greenfield, who gently and sincerely guided me through the most tumultuous times of my beginning, my awakening, my birth. She spent hours with me, joining me, affirming me, and helping me integrate my most intense experiences.

Dr. Crimi, who, upon my return home, after everything fell apart, took me under his giant wing, and gave me the tools and confidence I needed to move forward on my own path. He grabbed me by the ankles as I would float away and brought me solidly back down to earth.

Shizumi Crimi, who helped me develop the stick-to-it-iveness that I needed to ultimately finish this project. My most creative, practical and toughest friend! You, Shizumi, inspire me.

And finally, the one at the end who jumped in wholeheartedly and said YES to the vision, the mission, the destination: thank you, Rosalie Brown, for making this real.

As stated, there are so many not mentioned here. And I hope if you're reading this, and you don't see your name, you don't think that I didn't notice you, that I don't value you. I do. So very much.

In gratitude,

Ingrid Turner

INTRODUCTION

Welcome, my friend, to **Locked in Love**. This truly is a work of love and inspiration, and I'm honored to be the channel to bring forth such divine wisdom from Spirit. These messages are, as far as I understand, meant to inspire you and transform your thinking, so that you, dear friend, can allow the simple, profound magic of Divine Spirit to transform your whole life.

These messages came to me over days, weeks, months, and years. Every morning, I sit with Spirit, and ask for a message. Many of these messages are from that time of quiet. Others come to me at the most random intervals, like when I'm driving or doing dishes, and if I don't write them down quickly, they go away forever! That's the way channeling works – it's not mine. It comes through me, so it doesn't stay. Which has the added benefit of me getting as much out of this book as you!

Most of these messages are channeled from Monz, my Spirit Guide. He makes his appearance and shares wisdom, strength, and such simple Divine guidance. I also receive messages from YOUR guides, and what are commonly referred to as "Ascended Masters" – Mother Mary, Jesus, Ganesha, and others.

This book can be used in whatever way makes the most sense to you: you can read a message a day, or open to a random page for your daily guidance. You can use it like you would a divination tool: ask for guidance and open the book, and see what Spirit has for you. Please, use it however you like.

And if you'd like to share your process, I'd love to hear it! And so would the rest of the community, conveniently gathered on Facebook in the Living in Partnership with Spirit group.

So, new friend, enjoy this book. Enjoy these messages. Enjoy the transformation.

If you love this book, please consider leaving a review on Amazon. Your input will help with the updating of this piece, and future projects.

Much love,

Ingrid

INGRID TURNER

Have faith in your dreams.
You are on the right track.

Your throat chakra is very good for money magic.
The more you use it, the more you attract.

Focus and presence are the same thing.

Love your human experience.

Your desires are a signpost, not the destination.

Your desire is the form that you believe will give
you the feeling that you want. But your desire
limits what is possible for you. Sink into the feeling.
Let go of the form.

Your desires are given to you for a reason. They map out the path ahead for you. But don't get caught up in your desires being the end destination. They are not.

You cannot account for other people's perceptions.
Let that go, and trust in Me, trust in Us – all of this.

Follow your heart and you'll be surprised where your partner lands with it.

First and foremost, focus on your connection and
communion with Divine Spirit.
All else flows from there.

Invariably, during the process of awakening, your ego-self will clash with your expanding consciousness. This causes friction – crisis of faith, even. This is hard; it's painful. It is the shadow of your ego-self being ripped out of your new consciousness.

Trust the blocks.

Purpose is so far beyond comfortable.
It is an aliveness in your physical form that is
unmatched by anything else.

Just show up in every moment and
watch the magic happen.

Spirit is you, both as teacher and student: in a circle, reciprocating, reciprocating, reciprocating.

The feminine leads, the masculine follows. When the feminine is shining her light, the masculine knows where to go.
Without her shine, the masculine is lost.

Pursue with gusto what makes you happy. Let the pieces fall into place. You don't need to make any decisions right now. Just do what you love. When you pursue what you love, your life falls in to place. Every piece of it, with remarkably little effort.

It will always be, for now is forever.

You're not meant for everything, but you're meant
for more than you know.

The truth is,
you're going find your own way.

The stillness is so important.

When nothing is certain, it means everything is possible. If you demand certainty, you lose all that possibility. Sit here with me, then, in the uncertain abyss. Float with me across desolation. Breathe in the dark. Where can you go when you let go of that certain edge, and drift across the divide?

What if you didn't care?

Be brave in your love.

What happens when you wake up?
Chaos.

Remember that time doesn't exist. It's only divine moment to divine moment to divine moment. And every moment is perfect. You don't need to struggle with perfection.

Resisting even the uncomfortable, unpopular pieces of this whole messy human experience is what is keeping your dearest wishes at bay. Acknowledge and feel all of it. Do that now.

Feel the joy right now. Remember, presence is the key to all your dreams coming true. Right now! And if you're not seeing it now, it's because the skies are rearranging the stars for you.

Sometimes the most powerful way you
communicate is not with words,
but with energy.

I have heard you. We have heard you. All the cosmos has heard you.

Remain calm. When your nervous system fires too fast, you project so much energy into your environment that you're not able to control it. This lack of control frightens your brain, and that's when you start to spin out, and your energy goes where you don't want it to go.

You know that wide-open-feel-good-anything-is-possible space? Do you miss that space? Good, my dear. You're supposed to miss it. You're supposed to close off from it for a while, and then open back up to it and release the tautness. It is how you truly appreciate that space, of course, and it's also how you master that space. It's how you learn to stay relaxed in that space, and experience less and less of the tightening and constriction. It's like stretching your limbs and becoming flexible.

I hope you can sensually enjoy the process of
spiritual cleansing.

You are so loved. We miss you when you close off. But we know you don't mean to, and we'd never take it personally.

You are different. No better. No worse. The very best in your own light.

Slip back into the peace between activities. Like resting between contractions during the birthing process.

Find peace in the cracks of your life.

Every piece of experience is to be savored, dropped into. The divine is found in all of it. Fall. Don't hold yourself up any more. Let go. It's terrifying to let go. But remember: *every* experience is to be savored. You are the angel requesting the human experience. Now experience it!

You can't do a thing with those jumbles of thoughts
and feelings rattling in your body. Give them to us!
They are the special ingredients we use to make
the magic for you.

Don't be afraid to share. Don't be afraid of yourself. Don't be afraid of Me.

What fun would this grand journey be without
surprises? Relax. Rest.
It's easy now.

It's okay to ask!

Think of the bees. Busy, busy bees. But how busy are they? Busy and *focused.* One mission: the honey. The sweet stuff. Building everything towards the honey. The nectar.

What is *your* nectar? What sustains you?
Sweetness and goodness? Put all your mighty
focused effort into *that*.

It's frightening because it's expansion. And expansion stretches. And stretching, in the moment, is uncomfortable. Until you are more flexible. It's just like stretching your muscles and tendons. The same thing happens during your energetic expansion. Let go, and let it run its course. Everything is under control. All you have to do is wait. You can do that right? Wait. Easy.

Breathe into your heart.

It's a good, big, strong heart. Clear it out with your breath and intention.

Your heart is big, but not so big that you lose yourself in it. Don't let anyone make you feel that this is not a gift. It's one you've earned. It makes you strong.

Strong heart.

Keep clear with your breath.

To be taken care of, you have to feel taken care of.
Throw your head back. Smile. Laugh.
That's all there is.

Sometimes you get to do things just for the sake of doing it. No other reason.

Have some faith in yourself. You're evolving, changing, expanding. Trust yourself *in the moment*.

Your best bet is to not give it a thought until you get there.

Stay here with me today, and I promise you,
everything will work out wonderfully.

There is a crispness coming. At first, you might want to tighten your body against the cold air. Don't. Instead, relax into a new sensation and take interest in the change. It won't last long anyway.

You need to stop giving your power away. Some of
the ways you do this: accepting criticism,
identifying with other people's opinions, giving
yourself over to a teacher, group think, dogma,
and even accepting praise.

Spirit is coming through to you via your teacher.

Fear is merely the motivator to move. The direction is up to you.

Creation = LOVE

Everything is sound. A vibrational pitch. I like the term 'vibrational stance' because it takes the hierarchy out. To know your vibrational stance, ask someone to say your name. When they say your name, pay attention to where you feel the vibration along your chakras.
That is your vibrational stance in the moment.

We are the formless that take form to show you, show you, show you. Just to show you. It's just a reveal. And you grasp it so exquisitely because you already know, know, know.

Cosmos is being created, all inside of you.

You just keep doing what you do, and let it all come to you.

Just feel today.

What if you can decide what dimension you want to live in? It's not about "enough" people making a new decision. You can decide what world you want to live in. What keeps you here? Is it guilt? Love of drama? Lack of choice? Lack of faith? Honestly and rigorously identify, and then make the change.

If you wish.

You are fundamentally shifting your reality right now, and that cosmic shift inside of you rearranges the entire reality you live in. This means that some of the people in your reality will rearrange themselves on the same minute level. Some will journey with you, and some will not.

The more fun you have,
the more renowned you will be.

The anxiety you feel is part and parcel of the
activation process.
Let it run through your whole body.
It needs to touch every piece.

Never fear about next steps.
You, darling, are in no danger of complacency.

I know you don't feel at peace right now, but it's a long life. You don't need to be in the zone every minute of the rest of your life.

Where are you pulled?
Stop resisting that pull.

You've got to let go. It gets so easy when you do.
So easy!

If you're too sad to connect with Spirit, that's ok.
Because that is when Spirit is connected to You.
You just observe the sensation of the sadness. Find
the edges. You'll notice that it has an insulated
quality. There's a reason for that. Trust.

You forgot peace.

Fire symbolism: scorch that which you have been so unwilling to release.

When you experience a heartache, it is important
to express that energy so that it moves through
your body, and doesn't get all balled up and cause
problems. There are countless ways to express.
Complaining is just one of them.

Release the limits you put on yourself. Release them *all*.

Breathe. It all happens at the same pace. If you need to slow down, slow the breath. Enjoy. This life is glorious, even, and especially, in its madness.

If you want to shift the energy right now, trust yourself. Stop looking outside of Yourself for the balm, the salve, the relief. It all wells up inside of You when you *choose* to *trust yourself.* Trust is not earned. Trust is a choice.

The physical act of opening your arms and looking up opens your heart to all the possibilities, and your throat to express your joy.

A major contributing factor to a blocked throat chakra is not trusting yourself.

When we refer to you as "beautiful", it has nothing to do with your physical shape, tone, or size. We're reaching a finger into your heart and identifying the unending blissful state that is your right as a God being.

When you move aside the grief, blocks, resentments, injustices and pain that cover up your God essence, which is physically located in your heart space, you emanate radiant beauty that can be seen, felt, tasted, and fully, deeply experienced by everything you come into contact with; be that another human, an animal, an insect, a tree, a rock, oxygen, and even the smallest single atom.

Healing of *self* to unearth your God essence is the single most powerful thing you can do for the good of your planet. Really, it's the only thing. So, begin now: process, peel, heal, rise.

Humans and Spirit alike get into different 'modes' in order to energetically accomplish different tasks. It's okay to let that mode play out, even if it's not your preferred one.

Seeds are planted, and they sprout. When they sprout, leave them alone, so they can grow into sturdy saplings and then a big grove of trees. Leave the delicate sprouts alone!

When you allow yourself to rest, you allow Us to take care of you.

Everything is up and down, and it will always be up and down. And that's okay. Remember the divinity in all of it.

When you feel envy, it is because you are seeing someone stand in their power, and you are not standing in yours. You feel like they are stealing your power. But the truth is, they are just shining their own light. It's an indication that you need to step back into yours. When you are bright in your own light, you do not feel envy of others. Only joy at their success.

Keep expanding. Keep digging.
Keep doing you.

As Humans, you don't get to stay in the divine space all the time. When you accept those angst-y human places within yourself, and are at peace with the difficult side of yourself, you'll see the diamond gifts that are pouring out of you from those places.

Just be in your space,
however it shows up right now.
Action is not required.

You are not always here to make people feel good.

What if it's true?
What if you *are* that great?

The age of the Guru is over.

It doesn't have to happen immediately for it to be happening right now.

Anger is the energy that moves mountains.

To move mountains, SPEAK TRUTH.
No matter how uncomfortable.

Don't concern yourself with pleasing anybody.
Concern yourself with Truth.

Speaking Truth will break down every obstacle in your path.

Truth is not being nice. Truth is not kindness. You can speak truth without malice or ill intent. You can speak truth with compassion.
But Truth is not being kind.

Compassion is Truth. Action from compassion is Truth. But this is not the same as being kind. Kind holds back the Truth for fear of upsetting the bearer and the intended. Compassion speaks wholly and fully in Truth.

Responding to your desires is like responding to your name. When you hear your name called, it's compulsive to respond to it. Yet, you are not your name. Equally, you are not your desires.
But both are an integral part of your human experience.

Pause with the music.

Choose peace: stop when the music stops, dance when it plays again. Avoid all angst in this way.

The competitive spirit rises up in you to tell you that you can do much better. Discomfort comes when you compare your best to someone else's. You are not here to be the best at what they do. You are here to be the best at what you do.

Rest well in your *mind* and let your body take *relaxed actions*.

Relax first in your mind, and see how it all plays out!

Be present with your *growth*. When it's over, you'll realize it was the most delicious piece of all.

Sit where you are, and revel, revel with your heart.
Just because you're not there yet doesn't mean it's
not amazing now.

It's not about giving up.
It's about letting go.

I know it's uncomfortable right now. But that truly does not mean you are wrong, or bad, or displaced. You can rest right where you are, and then pick up again when you are well. It's not about pushing and shoving and crying tears of frustration.

It just doesn't have to be that way.

Lost is okay. Lost is wide open space. Lost is an opportunity to just be.

You don't have to name something to appreciate
its magnificence. You don't have to fully
understand it to EXPERIENCE it completely, fully,
breathtakingly. Be fully present in your experiences
by letting go of the need to understand them.
Understanding always comes. But let it go for the
moment so that you can have the full-body
pleasure of the thing.

We can give you the answers all day long. But it's up to you to get into alignment with them.

The spiritual journey goes from in to out and back again. Circles, figure eights, all connecting at ends and starts.

I can't control you.
I can only love you.

Each object, idea, feeling, breeze, and moment is a
Universe in and of itself.

The dark, difficult transformation process is sort of a forced grounding. Your God-selves are requiring you to dig deep, deep, deep into the black recesses of your human experiences, and that results in an elevated connection to Divine Spirit, along with an expanded human experience. Understood this way, the shadow becomes just as bright as the light. Just as bright.

Let go of the destination and you are free.

Empaths: the only way to eliminate your struggles in the world is to shine out unconditional love to all you meet and greet. Do this, and you'll feel every energy, emotion, sensation and vibration just as keenly as you always have, but you will be both protected, and finally, fully launched into the healer role, which is your whole purpose here on earth.

All those conditions you carry around your love aren't yours. They are human-made. They were created from words and suggestions and expectations. And can be uncreated just as easily.

Joy is such a key piece of your experience, darling. And it is one that so many of you don't embrace nearly as often as the opportunity presents itself.

Once you come to accept that everything and everyone is working in your favor, you see the possibilities everywhere. You notice the outstretched hand of God in every gesture. You see the twinkle of the Divine in every set of eyes. You hear the roar of Source in every laugh. You feel the quiet reassurance in every loss. You notice that messages, direction, and encouragement are smiling back at you from every angle, every which way you turn your attention. Now that you have accepted all is the gift, you grasp the hand, lock with the eyes, and smile in recognition of Divine intervention in all your life.

It's not about control. It's about empowerment.

And oddly, empowerment comes when you let go of control completely.

Judgment is what you use to cover up the nothingness you sense inside of you. Dive underneath the judgment, fall into the hollow space within, and find your bliss.

Get present and the answers will come.

There is not one, pre-determined path for your human experience. You experience every possible permutation of every moment in as many simultaneous dimensions as necessary.

You can't authentically express yourself until you authentically feel your feelings.

Do what you want in life, and do it with loving intent. Traversing the human experience with loving intent means you move in the direction of joy at an easy pace. That's it.
That's your whole purpose here.

Follow my heart
Speak my truth

Your life purpose is to be purposeful.

Do you want something? Stop pining for it. Intentionally place your energy there. Now you have it. It is done. Move on.

You are here to experience extreme contrast to your divine being, so that you may fall more deeply in love with who you are.

Only blind, crazy, innocent, naive love is going to make you strong for this life.

Just do love.

It's not about right and wrong. It's never about right and wrong. It's about love, and not love.

Dig deep enough and you find that peace is what you're after. And peace is presence. And presence experienced in this human form is divinity personified.

Breakthroughs come through breaking.

Enjoy! Enjoy! Enjoy! If you can remember that none of this is serious, no harm will come to you.

Resistance robs you of the fullness of your experience.

Let the moment be intensely, deliciously rich, and then let it go for the next one.

You take it all so seriously but; it's just a touch, just a breeze, just a second or two of rich experience.

Remind yourself every day to follow your heart and speak its truth. Otherwise you'll forget, and this world needs you to remember.

Bless you, uncomfortable
in-between space.

Take actions that keep you loving
your life.

Self mastery comes through self love.

'Flow' means going with your impulses.

It's okay to acknowledge when things are hard. When you acknowledge it, you can release it, and that moves the resistance through. Ego identity creates resistance. But in your effort to avoid identifying with your hardship, you can inadvertently create another ego identity which secures the same resistance. It is so important to feel all of the emotions that arise within you. This is your stunning human experience.

Laughter is the antidote to all your blocks.

Keep getting uncomfortable.

Your energy takes the shape of the stories you
create.

Your life purpose is to be purposeful.

Release all the baggage you've been carrying around. You betray no one by releasing the weight of other people's expectations, judgments, and projections.

When you're in love with your mission, divine timing won't bother you.

You don't want the thing you want.
You want the feeling you believe that thing will
provide you.

You are so powerful.

Ego identity creates resistance.

Resist the urge to take responsibility for someone else's response to anything.
Tempting to think you have that kind of power, isn't it?

Just because you understand and empathize with someone's experience doesn't mean you have to stick around for it.

Let God blow your mind.

Gratitude equals love. Fall in love today.

Intention and prayer are the same thing.

Stay calm in the moment. Come back to self. Focus on energy. Every time. Right here in the moment: this is where all your success is.

Heal yourself by whatever means necessary.

The more you relax into life, the more you can create during your time here.

Everything is a message. You have ears to hear, eyes to see, fingers to touch, and a heart to understand.

How do you stop caring about what other people think? Love them.

ABOUT THE AUTHOR

Ingrid is an author, minister, psychic medium, and spiritual teacher. She uses the modalities of psychic intuition and mediumship to express the Divine. In addition to acting as a channel to Divine Spirit for groups and individuals, she founded the *Bhava Spiritual Mission*, a not-for-profit organization dedicated to helping people connect directly with the infinite. The Bhava Spiritual Mission has multiple arms, including a ministry to teach people how to connect to Divine Spirit and build their spiritual business, and a publishing division, helping spiritual teachers from all walks of life share their message and their light.

You can learn more about Ingrid on her website: *ingridhturner.com*, and more about the Bhava Spiritual Mission at *bhavamission.org*

CPSIA information can be obtained
at www.ICGtesting.com
Printed in the USA
FSHW010851030319
56064FS